CW00996663

Contents

Kathryn Sturrock is mother to four children, which is how her crafting journey began. As each of her children left to go to full time school, Kathryn decided to take up a new hobby – crafting with polymer clay. She now describes herself as a self-confessed craftaholic!

Kathryn began making gifts, picture frames, cake toppers and card embellishments. She soon discovered that many people were interested in purchasing her work, so Kathryn started her own business, Karacter Krafts by Kathryn. After a number of years, the business had picked up pace dramatically, so she opened her first shop in Doncaster, South Yorkshire at the end of August 2008. A couple of premises moves later, with a roller coaster ride of highs and lows along the way, Kathryn found herself guest presenting on TV's Create & Craft channel.

Throughout, Kathryn continued to make cute and whimsical clay characters under the brand name Sugar Buttons™.

Kathryn was first introduced to Katy Sue Designs® when she was asked to jointly guest present some of their TV shows with Christina Ludlam, Katy Sue's very talented sugar craft artist and cake designer. Using the fantastic Katy Sue Designs® moulds and design mats, she introduced new ways of creating embellishments for paper crafters and found a new love for a different type of clay, air drying clay.

Kathryn's love for all things clay soon became apparent to Create & Craft TV and the popular Crafting With Clay TV shows were launched. Katy Sue Designs® then approached Kathryn to collaborate in turning her character designs into moulds. With the release of the first set of Sugar Buttons™ characters, Kathryn is delighted to be able to share some of the Sugar Buttons™ family with you and the many crafters out there.

Now you have the ability to make Kathryn's cute little people and use them on your craft, home décor, cake or paper craft projects time and time again.

The first release of moulds and this project book is the start of a new and exciting journey for Kathryn and Sugar Buttons™.

Katy Sue Designs® are manufacturers and designers of imaginative craft products. Their product range crosses over cake decorating, general crafts and papercrafts and include highly detailed moulds, patented tools and stamps, as well as the Flower Soft® range of craft sprinkles.

The award winning moulds from Katy Sue are known for their intricate detail and ease of use, making them very popular with cake decorators, card makers, jewellery artists, crafters and mixed media enthusiasts. The Katy Sue moulds encompass many different styles and are manufactured at their own factory in the north east of England.

Retailers around the world stock this unique product range and the Katy Sue Designs® brands are regularly seen on craft TV in the UK and USA.

INTRODUCTION

Air drying clays can be found in a lightweight form, paper clay which you can purchase in white or coloured blocks, cold porcelain, which is usually purchased as an off-white colour (you can add your own colour to it), air drying polymer clay (similar to cold porcelain but extremely strong) or a heavier weight basic clay such as DAS (which often dries to a greyish colour).

When it comes to the use of moulds and especially the high quality of the very detailed Katy Sue Designs® moulds, you may find lightweight air drying clays (paper clays) more appropriate. For the air drying clay projects in this book, I have used the brand Hearty Clay. It is strong, versatile and very light so it is suitable for a whole host of projects including paper crafting. It will not weigh down your cards and won't cost the earth if posting.

The white clay can be mixed with coloured clay to create endless combinations and shades, or alternatively you can add colour in other ways such as inks, gel food colouring and acrylic paint. You can also paint directly onto the dried white clay once your project is made.

Before we start the process of creating a character from the moulds, below is a list of items you will need:

- **Sugar Buttons™ character mould**
- **White air drying clay**
- **A glass cutting mat or chopping board** (smooth surface)
- **A tool of your choice** to aid pushing the clay into delicate parts of the mould. A sugar crafter's tool is ideal for this type of clay
- **A metal or acrylic rolling pin**
- **A selection of acrylic paints** (including a skin colour)
- **Cornflour and a powder brush** (for dusting your moulds)
- **Wet wipes** for cleaning hands and clay in-between colour changes

PREPARATION

The Hearty air dry clay comes in a sealed foil pack. On first opening, it will be quite wet to touch, but not sticky, and feels like marshmallow. As the air gets to the clay, it will begin to dry out quite quickly. Keep any clay that you are not using in a sealed, air free bag.

It is useful to keep a wet wipe to hand to cover any bits of clay that you are working on, to stop it drying out too quickly. This said, I prefer not to use air drying clays straight from the pack into the mould as they are often quite wet and sticky when first opened, which will make the clay stick and be difficult to release. Work the clay in your hands and if very wet place against a paper towel until all excess moisture is removed. To aid with the release from the mould, dust the mould with a little cornflour, tapping out any excess before adding the clay. You will soon get to know the feel of the clay. As it starts to dry out a little, you will feel it becoming firmer.

At first you will need a few attempts to get a perfect result, so if you find that the clay sticks a little in the mould, just take it out and use a ball of the clay to push back into the mould and grab any loose bits of clay that has stuck inside. Begin the process again, you can re-use the clay until it dries out and starts to harden or form lumps. Once it dries out, it will be unusable, so keep spare clay air tight and free from dust and contamination.

If you are a complete beginner with any type of clay and moulds, start with the air drying clay method first, until you gain experience and confidence with the moulds.

To gauge how much clay you will use for each mould, take a piece of clay and push it into your chosen mould until it fills the shape to the top of the rim. The clay can now be removed.

For your first attempt using air drying clay with a mould, follow this tutorial to make a Ballerina.

1. Prepare your mould by dusting with cornflour and tapping out any excess.

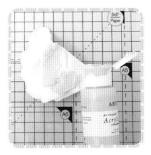

2. Use skin coloured acrylic paint, gel food colouring, ink, or powder paint to add to white clay to form a skin tone colour. Mix the colouring well into the clay by folding and stretching the clay, until it forms an even colour. Using acrylic paint may make your clay a little more wet and sticky, so allow the clay to sit on a paper towel to dry for a short time before using.

3. Roll coloured clay into a smooth ball or sausage shape ready to apply to your mould.

4. Push the clay into the mould with your fingertips, making sure that you get into all detailed parts. Keep any posts that appear in the mould to create space (eg. between legs) free from clay.

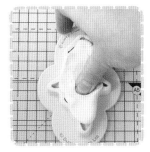

5. Fill the mould to the rim and remove any excess clay, by pushing excess to one side and pinching off between your fingers.

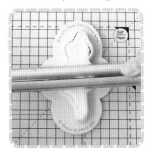

6. Use a rolling pin to flatten the clay by rolling across the top of the mould. This will ensure that the clay is well packed into the detailed areas.

7. Use a finger to pull the clay inwards slightly from the edges of the mould. This will give a neat edge to your character and help the release of the figure.

Flex the mould, gently away from the clay edges all the way around the figure and ease the figure upwards to lift out of the mould. If you have difficulty with this method, turn over the mould and start to ease the clay figure downwards by flexing the mould backwards with your fingers, taking care not to squash the character.

The character should ease out onto your surface. If your first attempt isn't perfect roll up and try again, it may take a couple of attempts to get used to handling the mould.

8. Leave on a flat paper towel to dry completely. You should allow up to 24 hours to dry thoroughly. Most air drying clays will shrink a little as they dry out, as the clay loses its moisture. The detail in the characters will stay perfectly intact, despite some shrinkage.

9. Once the air dry clay figure has thoroughly dried, add a coat of clear drying glue/sealant over the entire figure, then a coat of gesso or white paint to the non-skin tone areas of the figure to form a good base for your colours, you can now paint the hair and clothing and eye recesses with black or dark brown paint. For instructions on the method of adding clay eyes see Using Polymer Clay With Moulds section.

INTRODUCTION

Polymer clay is a very versatile clay. It is an oven bake clay, that does not require specialist equipment, just a standard home oven, a few tools and accessories. Polymer clay contains plasticisers, so basically it is a plastic clay. It is non-toxic and can be used in a wide variety of ways, from creating fun models to magnificent sculptured, detailed pieces. You can create objects freehand, or with the help of moulds. Polymer clay holds detail well, as it is quite a firm clay. It is not air drying, so you can put it to one side and return later if you don't finish a project. Polymer clay can be used by children and adults alike. Always check the packaging of each individual brand for guidelines and suggested age ability and use.

If you are new to polymer clay, using good quality moulds is a great place to start.

With the first range of **Sugar Buttons**™ characters, made in conjunction with **Katy Sue Designs**®, you can make cute, whimsical characters with their own unique characteristics. They will open up a range of opportunities to use the characters over and over again on your craft projects. Whether you are a paper crafter, sugar craft artist, cake maker, someone who enjoys home décor projects or making handmade gifts, these moulds are ideal. The possibilities are endless, as you can change colours and details for each creation.

Before we start the process of creating a character from the moulds, below is a list of items you will need:

- **Sugar Buttons**™ **character mould**
- **Polymer clay** in your chosen colours
- **A glass cutting mat or chopping board** (smooth surface)
- **A tool of your choice** to aid pushing the clay into delicate parts of the mould. This could be a sugar crafter's tool, a polymer clay specialist tool, dentistry tools (widely used in candle making, clay and other crafts), a small to medium ball tool or even a round ended paintbrush may work
- **A metal or acrylic rolling pin**
- **A clay roller machine, or pasta machine** (optional)
- **A filled and covered hot water bottle** (optional)
- **Wet wipes** for cleaning hands and clay in-between colour changes

PREPARATION

Before filling the mould you need to condition the clay. This is done by rolling the clay colours individually through a clay roller or pasta machine, or by rolling backwards and forwards on a glass mat and between the palms of your hands until the clay becomes soft and pliable.

This is where your optional hot water bottle comes in! Sit the clay on a hot water bottle and the gentle heat will begin the softening process and speed up the conditioning of the clay. Polymer clay bakes with heat, so DO NOT place uncured clay on anything too hot, or in direct heat before you have moulded as it will become unusable.

To check if clay is conditioned enough, roll a sausage of clay and bend backwards and forwards. If it is nice and pliable, the clay is ready for use. If it cracks and breaks easily, continue to condition the clay further.

The mould does not require any preparation, except washing with soapy water the first time you use it. Make sure that the mould is thoroughly dry before adding clay.

Polymer clay can be easily painted with acrylic paints after baking, however the method below shows how to build up the clay colours in a sequence within the mould. With practice, you will learn the best sequence for adding the colours.

Follow this tutorial for your first attempt. You may find that you can adapt these instructions to suit yourself as you go along, but on most occasions, it really does matter which order you add the coloured clay. Remember, as you fill the mould, you are looking at it from the back. It is only when you release the character from the mould that you will see the benefit of how you have added the clay and the full detail.

1. Start with black clay for the boots and waistcoat of the Pirate. Roll a sausage of clay and push into the feet first and follow up to the top of the boot.

Keep within the outlines of each area by pushing in place with your fingers or your chosen tool. Make sure they clay is applied thinly as if you overfill the areas you will find that the colours bleed together as you add more clay. If this happens you can roll the clay back into a ball and start again.

Do not add the black clay eye-patch at this stage. The hair needs to be created first, so we will come back to the eye-patch shortly.

2. Next add clay which creates the hair. Make sure that you push the clay well into the detailed areas, without overfilling. Pay particular attention to the fringe and small amounts of hair around the ears and neck.

The black eye-patch can now be added by adding a small thin piece of clay into the outlined area. Once again DO NOT OVERFILL otherwise you will find that your released pirate is wearing a mask rather than an eye-patch!

3. Next add the red bandanna. Once again, push the clay within the outlines of the area you are filling. I find that it helps to 'slope' the clay slightly to avoid overfilling. You can also add clay for the shirt in this way. The white clay I have used has totally covered the black waistcoat and has been shaped with my tool to stop at the points of the hands, neckline and trousers.

4. Now add the skin coloured clay. Roll small balls of clay for each hand and push into position. The head of each character has simple and small facial features. Be sure to roll a ball of skin coloured clay until it is warm and smooth. Push it directly into the mould with your fingers to ensure that the clay goes into these delicate parts.

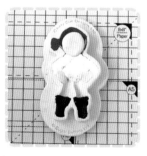

5. Add the Pirate's trousers, then flatten and smooth the surface of the clay by rolling with a rolling pin. If you need to 'top up' the clay at this point, you can do so now. Don't worry if the clay colours are blending together at this point. The clay beneath is being pushed firmly into all of the tiny detailed areas

below and you will be amazed at how it looks when you release the character from the mould.

When you are completely happy that the clay has filled the mould and is smooth, flat and level with the outer rim of the mould, the clay filling process is complete.

6. Use a finger to pull the clay inwards slightly from the edges of the mould. This will give a neat edge to your character and help on the release of the figure. Each mould has a unique 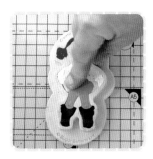 'lip' around its outer edge which will also help to flex and release. Don't be afraid to flex the mould well. It will not break. You can use it over and over without fear of it falling apart.

 As you pull down the outer lip of the mould, gently start to ease the clay figure upwards with your fingers, taking care not to squash the character, alternatively turn the mould over and flex backwards allowing the figure to ease out onto the surface. When you release the feet of the character, try to ease out the clay in line with the mould to avoid excessive bending.

7. Roll a tiny ball of white clay and pick up with a small ball tool (metal embossing tool). You can use this tool to place the white of the eyes on your character, by pressing very gently into  place. The eye will take on a slightly rounded shape by using this tool, which is ideal.

8. Add an even smaller ball of black clay in the same way to the eye socket. Use a toothpick dipped in white paint to add a glint of light to the eye. Alternatively, paint in the eye detail with acrylic paint, once your character has been cured in the oven. You will be surprised how the face now takes on character!

9. You can add some rosy cheeks to your characters face too, by dusting on some chalk or blush with a small sponge applicator. He's really coming to life now and is ready for the final details.

10. You can add coloured stripes directly into the mould as you fill it. Alternatively, roll thin pieces of red clay and cut into strips to add to the Pirate's shirt to create  stripes. Some may find this easier than trying to add the striped effect straight into the mould.

Of course, you could also paint the stripes with acrylic paint once the figure has been in the oven.

11. Bake your figure in the oven as per the instruction on your polymer clay packaging.

Adding further details, such as buttons on his waistcoat, or a gloss varnish for shiny boots, waistcoat and eye, will add character and style to your figure.

PROJECT 1:

Fairy Wishes Gift Bag

1. Mix a skin coloured air drying clay (as per instructions on page 2) and add to your Fairy mould. Flex, release and allow to dry thoroughly.

2. Add a coat of clear drying glue/sealant to the figure, then add a coat of gesso or white paint to form a good base on the non-flesh parts of the figure, allowing each coat to dry thoroughly.

3. Begin painting the fairy and add any extra details required. Continue by building up the paint colours on the hair, flowers, wings and eyes. Add a second coat of paint if required and allow to dry thoroughly.

4. You can continue to add fine detail with alcohol pens, on areas such as the hair and dress, to highlight detail and shading.

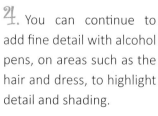

5. Once the fairy is complete, set aside whilst you make the gift bag. It takes a relatively small amount of card or paper, but the final trimmings are up to you.

Choose a good weight of decorative double sided paper for this project, so that the gift bag will be just as pretty inside as out. I used 250gsm. Cut the paper to a size of 28cm x 21cm (11 x 8 ¼ inches).

6. The example shows plain white paper with markings to show where to score and fold lines, to demonstrate the steps taken. You will of course follow these steps by using your decorative double sided paper cut to size.

Place your piece of paper landscape orientation on a large scoreboard, (if you only have an A4 sized scoreboard, use a ruler and pencil to mark the measurements and then score separately).

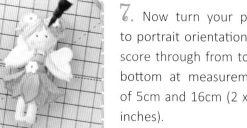

Score through from top to bottom, at measurements of 2cm, 11.5cm, 16.5cm and 26cm (¾, 4 ½ , 6 ½, 10 ¼ inches).

7. Now turn your paper to portrait orientation and score through from top to bottom at measurements of 5cm and 16cm (2 x 6 ⅓ inches).

8. Use a scoring tool or bone folder to crease well each score line both ways, so that the folds are flexible.

9. Turn your paper to landscape again and measure and mark with a pencil, a faint dot in the middle at 2.5cm (1 inch) of the two central vertical score lines.

Also pencil a faint dot 5cms (2 inches) away from the opposite sides of the central vertical score lines.

Mark these dots on the edge of the card on both top and bottom as both edges will be treated the same.

10. You are now going to score diagonally from the cross over points of your central horizontal and vertical score lines, to each dot you have marked.

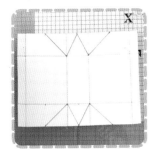

To make this clear, the example shows these lines drawn. It will form a 'W' shape within this area.

You need to do the same on both edges of your card, as shown.

11. With your paper placed portrait way on a flat surface and the desired inside pattern face up, fold the two edges inwards.

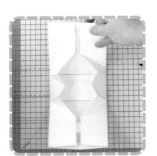

12. Following the diagonal score lines, begin to create the opening which forms the base of your gift bag. If you have folded along the score lines correctly, you should find that when you close your gift bag

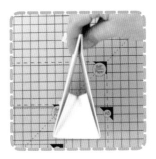

together, the base of the bag will form with a neat tucked edge each side. The front and back of the gift bag should have a nice flat surface to decorate.

13. Add ribbon or string handles if desired. Add glue or double sided tape right across the width of the paper above the score lines closest to both edges and attach two equal lengths of ribbon or string next to the vertical score lines on each edge.

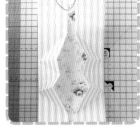

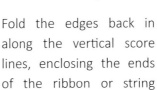

Fold the edges back in along the vertical score lines, enclosing the ends of the ribbon or string handles and stick down firmly with the glue or tape.

DO NOT add any extra glue or tape, other than that instructed.

14. Trim your gift bag by attaching your Sugar Buttons™ Fairy, ribbon, gems or other embellishments to complete your design. You can paint and glitter a little peg and added a paper clay flower made from the Katy Sue Designs® Little Flowers mould, to form a closure for your bag. Attach a note or sentiment with the peg too.

Why not make a number of these gift bags to use as party favours, teachers gifts, Bridesmaids gifts, Mothers Day or Easter treats? They make the perfect gift for any occasion!

PROJECT 2:

Ballerina Picture Frame

1. With your glass mat, chosen tool and the Ballerina Sugar Buttons™ mould to hand, you are now ready to create another lovely project. Choose your polymer clay colours and condition the clay in preparation to adding to the mould.

Start by adding clay to the roses on the dress and in the hair, and also the main part of the Ballerina's shoes. The finer detail of the shoe straps will added later.

2. Next add the hair. Be careful not to miss the small strands around the ears and neckline.

3. Add the dress, keeping within the detail lines of the mould and making sure not to overlap the head, arm and leg areas.

4. Next add the skin tone colour. Make sure that the clay is well softened and rolled into a smooth ball before adding the head, to ensure that the clay picks up the fine detail in the face.

5. Roll over the back of the mould with your rolling pin to ensure that the clay is pushed into all of the detailed areas. If you need to top up the mould, you can do so and roll again until the clay is level with the edges of the mould giving a smooth even surface.

6. Release the Ballerina figure carefully from the mould as the instructions on page 5.

7. Fill the eye area with a tiny amount of white and black clay. It is surprising how much this step adds to the character the face.

8. Next, roll out a thin piece of clay, the same colour as the shoes and cut strips to the width of the straps. Carefully add these over the appropriate area and cut to size, gently pressing in place. (You could have added this when filling the mould if you like fiddly bits!)

For extra detail, add a band of clay to the Ballerina's waist.

9. Your Ballerina is now ready for the oven. Once the figure has been cured, allow to cool down completely, before adding any glitter or paint as required.

10. Choose a small recessed frame, to allow further detail in the background. These frames are widely available, often in natural wood or pre-painted.

11. Create a background by colouring air dry clay (Hearty White) with food colouring. Squeeze a little colouring and fold into the clay. Keep stretching and folding until the colouring has mixed in fully to create a solid colour ready for use.

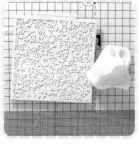

12. Try the Romantic Swirl design mat from Katy Sue Designs®. Dust with cornflour, tapping out any excess. Lightly roll out your coloured air dry clay to about the thickness of a coin and then lay this over the mat. Press rolled

clay gently onto the surface of the mat, so that it has a 'bite'. Roll out further with your rolling pin until you can just start to see the pattern beginning to show through the clay and covering the surface of the design mat. Peel away the clay from the mat, revealing the beautiful texture.

13. Take the part of the frame which forms the recess and place over your textured clay. Cut away any excess with a craft knife, **remembering that there will be some shrinkage** and allow the clay to dry.

14. Once dry, glue to the back plate of the frame and glue the recess framework in place.

15. Decorate the inside of your frame with anything that is not deeper than the recess. The frame makes a

lovely 3D picture for a room and can be decorated to a theme of your choice.

Try the Bunting Alphabet design mat from Katy Sue Designs® to add a name.

16. To finish off the edge of your frame, add lace trims. Be careful not to choose something too wide that may hide the elements inside the frame.

17. Put all of the pieces of the frame together. Glue your Ballerina figure to the outside of the frame and add any further embellishments, such as a ribbon bow or gems.

to allow an overlap on the inside. Stick the paper up to the edge of the spiral bound spine of the book, front and back. Be sure to stick the paper down smoothly and trim off any excess areas to make a neat flat finish on both the inside and outside covers.

6. Choose a contrasting paper and cut two pieces slightly smaller than the covers. Stick in place on the inner side of both covers to hide the raw edges and give a neat finish inside and out.

7. Add a delicate lace trim and pearl edging strip along the edge of the spiral binding. You can see on the example where the original colour of the notebook remains on show, as the paper covering can only go as far as the spiral binding. Choose two colours of decorative ribbon. Tie alternating colours to each spiral and trim to the desired length.

PROJECT 3:

Princess Memory Book

1. Mix a skin coloured air drying clay (as per instructions on page 2) and add to your Princess mould. Flex, release and allow to dry thoroughly.

2. Once the air dry clay figure has thoroughly dried, add a coat of clear drying glue/sealant and a coat of gesso or white paint to the non skin tone areas of the figure to form a good base for your colours.

3. Begin to paint the dress in your choice of colour. Continue to add colour to the princess's hair, shoes, ribbon, collar, crown and eyes. Add a second coat of paint if necessary and allow to dry thoroughly.

4. Choose a spiral bound notebook with a hard cover, which has a colour to compliment your theme, as a small amount of the original cover will remain visible.

5. Cut two pieces of decorative paper, approx ½ inch / 1 cm larger than the front and back covers,

8. Use the Katy Sue Designs® Oval Hearts decorative plaque mould to create a base for the Princess. You can use either air drying clay or polymer clay for this step. Make sure that the clay fills the mould and is rolled smooth and flat with your rolling pin. Flex the mould and release the plaque.

If using polymer clay, cure in the oven and allow to cool completely, or if using air drying clay, make sure that it is thoroughly dried out before gluing to the front cover of your book.

9. Glue your Sugar Buttons™ Princess onto the plaque and add and finishing detail such as glitter or gems to her dress. You can apply all kinds of embellishments to the front cover of your book, such as a name or sentiment.

A perfect gift fit for any Princess!

1. Mix a skin coloured air drying clay (as per instructions on page 2) and add to your Pirate mould. Flex, release and allow to dry thoroughly.

2. Seal the dried clay with a coat of clear drying glue/ sealant and then paint the non skin tone areas with gesso or white paint to give a good base for your colour application. Allow to dry.

3. Once dry, begin painting the colours of the Pirate's clothing and the finer details. Add stripes to the shirt and any other detail desired. Complete with a second coat of paint. Carefully paint in the eye detail, to give your Sugar Buttons™ Pirate real character. Allow the paint to dry thoroughly.

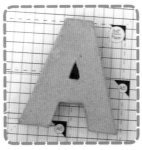

4. Choose a shape for your project. Many shapes are readily available as papier maché, MDF or wood. Paint your shape with gesso or emulsion as an undercoat and then apply two coats of your chosen colour and allow to dry.

Add white spots to your letter shape. Instead of painting them, try using a hole punch to create lots of spots in uniform size and glue them to the surface with a clear drying PVA. Add a clear coat of glue/ sealant if required once all spots have dried.

5. Glue your pirate figure in place. Add a length of brown garden string to your shape, where the wording will go. Tie two pieces of knotted ribbon to each end of the 'rope'.

6. Use the Katy Sue Designs® Bunting Alphabet design mat to make clay flags and stick in place to spell the word 'AHOY'. You can use either polymer clay, or air dry clay to make the flags in your own colour choice. Highlight raised areas of the flags with acrylic paint.

7. Finally, paint in any further details required and add matt or gloss varnish to any parts that need extra protection or shine.

Your finished wall art will look shipshape as a single initial on a bedroom door. Or make a number of letters in this way to spell out a child's name or a word for a pirate themed bedroom.

PROJECT 5:

Ballerina Keepsake Card

1. Mix a skin coloured air drying clay (as per instructions on page 2) and add to your Ballerina mould. Flex, release and allow to dry thoroughly.

2. Add a coat of clear drying glue/sealant and a coat of gesso or white paint to the non skin tone areas of your Ballerina to form a good base for your colours.

3. Begin to paint the dress, shoes, hair, roses and eye detail of your figure. Add a second coat of paint if required to cover sufficiently. Allow to dry thoroughly.

4. Choose two folded card blanks, measuring 4 ½ inches (11.5cm) square and 3 ½ inches (9cm) square. They will form the base structure.

5. Fold one half of each square card top to the centre fold line, as shown in the example.

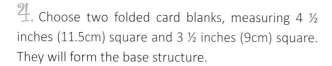

6. Cut a 4 ½ inch (11.5cm) and 3 ½ inch (9cm) square piece of card in the same colour

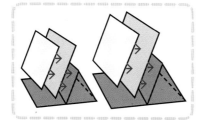

as your base cards. Now cut smaller squares in ¼ inch (0.5cm) increments using contrasting patterned or coloured paper squares for each base card and layer them up with smallest on top so they create a framed effect. Attach both layered squares to their corresponding base front below the folded line as shown on the example. Add a piece of lace trim to the smaller card face.

7. Stick both card bases together. The front card is smaller, so centralise it across the width of the larger back card and place the fold line of the smaller card halfway down the base of the larger back card. The front card forms a stopper for the larger back card to sit against.

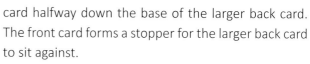

8. Glue your completed Sugar Buttons™ Ballerina to the face of the front card.

9. Create a small raised plaque with card and foam dots to make a 'stopper' at the front base of the card, so that your Ballerina can stand properly and will not slide forward.

10. Use the Bunting Alphabet design mat from Katy Sue Designs® to create wording on the back card. Add glitter, gems and embellishments of your choice to both front and back layers and build up a little 'stage' for your ballerina.

Why not trim your box to match. It will make a stunning gift right on pointe!